INSIDE YOUR BODY

ALL ABOUT SORE THROATS

FRANCESCA POTTS, RN

Consulting Editor, Diane Craig, MA/Reading Specialist

Super Sandcastle

An Imprint of Abdo Publishing
abdopublishing.com

ABDOPUBLISHING.COM

Published by Abdo Publishing, a division of ABDO, PO Box 398166, Minneapolis, Minnesota 55439. Copyright © 2018 by Abdo Consulting Group, Inc. International copyrights reserved in all countries. No part of this book may be reproduced in any form without written permission from the publisher. Super SandCastle™ is a trademark and logo of Abdo Publishing.

Printed in the United States of America,
North Mankato, Minnesota
062017
092017

Production: Mighty Media, Inc.
Editor: Megan Borgert-Spaniol
Cover Photographs: iStock, Shutterstock
Interior Photographs: iStock, Shutterstock

Publisher's Cataloging-in-Publication Data
Names: Potts, Francesca, author.
Title: All about sore throats / by Francesca Potts, RN.
Description: Minneapolis, MN : Abdo Publishing, 2018. I Series:
    Inside your body
Identifiers: LCCN 2016962913 I ISBN 9781532111204 (lib. bdg.) I
    ISBN 9781680789058 (ebook)
Subjects: LCSH: Throat--Diseases--Juvenile literature.
Classification: DDC 616.3--dc23
LC record available at http://lccn.loc.gov/2016962913

Super SandCastle™ books are created by a team of professional educators, reading specialists, and content developers around five essential components—phonemic awareness, phonics, vocabulary, text comprehension, and fluency—to assist young readers as they develop reading skills and strategies and increase their general knowledge. All books are written, reviewed, and leveled for guided reading, early reading intervention, and Accelerated Reader™ programs for use in shared, guided, and independent reading and writing activities to support a balanced approach to literacy instruction.

CONTENTS

YOUR BODY

YOUR THROAT

You're amazing! So is your body.

Most of the time your body works just fine. It lets you go to school, play with friends, and more. But sometimes you feel sick or part of you hurts.

A sore throat is one way your body can hurt. Sore throats are common when you are sick. It can be painful to swallow. It is even hard to yawn!

WHAT IS A
SORE
THROAT?

Your throat is a **passageway**. It leads to two different tubes. One lets air pass from the mouth to the lungs. The other sends food and liquid to the stomach.

MOUTH

THROAT

TRACHEA
(TUBE TO LUNGS)

LUNGS

ESOPHAGUS
(TUBE TO STOMACH)

STOMACH

A sore throat is usually a **symptom** of an **infection**. The infection can make your throat feel dry or raw. You may also have a stuffy nose or cough. These symptoms can make a sore throat feel even worse!

{ **FAST FACT** }

The medical term for the throat is pharynx (*FAIR-inks*).

BACTERIAL INFECTION

CAUSES

There are several causes that can lead to a sore throat.

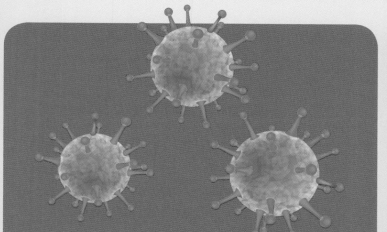

Viruses

Viruses are a type of **germ**. They need to be inside living things to survive. Humans are often their hosts! Viruses cause illnesses. They cause the flu and common cold.

Bacteria

Bacteria are another kind of germ. They can spread in or outside of the body. Bacteria cause illnesses such as strep throat.

Air Quality

Breathing dry or smoky air can cause a sore throat. So can air that is high in **allergens**.

Muscle Strain

Shouting can strain the muscles of your throat. So can talking for a long time. This makes your throat sore.

SIGNS AND SYMPTOMS

THINK OF THE LAST TIME YOU HAD A SORE THROAT. DID YOU HAVE OTHER SYMPTOMS TOO?

COUGHING

SNEEZING

Most sore throats are caused by viruses. They often come with the **symptoms** of a common cold.

RUNNY NOSE

LOW ENERGY

HEADACHE

SORE THROAT OR STREP THROAT?

Has your sore throat lasted longer than a day or two? Does it come with more severe **symptoms**? You may have strep throat.

Strep throat is an **infection**. It is caused by bacteria called *Streptococci*. You should see a doctor if you think you have strep throat.

Sore Throat

CAUSE: Usually a virus

SYMPTOMS: Coughing, sneezing, runny nose, headache, fever, reduced smell and taste

TREATMENT: Pain medicine or home remedies

Strep Throat

CAUSE: Bacteria

SYMPTOMS: Fever, swollen **glands**, red throat with white spots, stomach pain

TREATMENT: **Antibiotics**

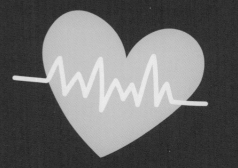

Strep throat can lead to more serious problems. Rheumatic fever is an illness that affects the heart. It can occur when strep throat is not treated correctly.

ILLNESSES

Other illnesses can cause a sore throat. Have you ever been sick with one of these?

TONSILLITIS is an **infection** of the tonsils. These are the two lumps in the back of your throat. They fight off **germs** that enter your mouth and nose.

RED TONSILS WITH WHITE OR YELLOW SPOTS

SORE THROAT

BAD BREATH

FEVER

EAR PAIN

MONO is short for *mononucleosis*. This virus spreads through **saliva**. Mono makes you feel very tired for several weeks.

FEVER

SORE THROAT

ACHING MUSCLES

TIREDNESS

LOSS OF APPETITE

FEVER

RUNNY NOSE

SORE THROAT

COUGH THAT SOUNDS LIKE A BARK

CROUP is caused by a virus. It affects the upper airways. Croup mostly occurs in small children. But older kids can get it too.

WARNING

Most sore throats can be treated at home. But take note if you start to feel worse! Here are a few signs that you should see a doctor:

Sore throat that lasts more than a week

Hard to swallow or breathe

Yellow **pus** in the back of throat

Tiredness that lasts more than a week

GOING TO
THE DOCTOR

You might decide to see a doctor about your sore throat. The doctor will ask you about your **symptoms**. Then she or he may do a few tests. This will show what is causing the sore throat.

- The doctor may feel your neck to check for swollen **glands**.

- The doctor will use a special flashlight to look at the back of your throat.

- The doctor can listen to your lungs.

- The doctor may swipe the back of your throat with a cotton swab. This test will show if you have strep throat.

TREATMENT

Most sore throats go away on their own. It will take about a week for you to feel better. But there are things you can do to help your body fight!

- Get lots of rest.

- Drink water, hot tea, and juice.

- Avoid soda and other drinks with **caffeine**.

- Take medicines to ease pain and clear your stuffy nose.

CARE FOR YOUR THROAT! HERE ARE A FEW REMEDIES FOR A SORE THROAT:

Hot water with lemon and honey

Cool or frozen treats

Throat drops and sprays

Gargling with salt water

PREVENTION

Sore throats happen when **germs** spread between people. Sometimes this is hard to avoid. But you can still do your best to keep germs away!

AVOID SHARING CUPS, FORKS, AND SPOONS WITH OTHERS.

AVOID FAMILY AND FRIENDS WHO HAVE SORE THROATS.

COVER YOUR NOSE AND MOUTH
WHEN YOU COUGH OR SNEEZE.

WASH YOUR HANDS! THIS IS THE
BEST WAY TO STOP THE SPREAD
OF GERMS.

GLOSSARY

ALLERGEN – something that causes an allergic reaction.

ANTIBIOTIC – a substance used to kill germs that cause disease.

CAFFEINE – a substance that makes you feel more awake.

GERM – a tiny, living organism that can make people sick.

GLAND – an organ in the body that makes chemicals that your body needs.

INFECTION – an unhealthy condition caused by bacteria or other germs.

PASSAGEWAY – any path or way through which something can pass.

PUS – a thick, yellowish substance the body produces when it has an infection.

SALIVA – a liquid produced in the mouth.

SYMPTOM – a noticeable change in the normal working of the body.